The DRAGON'S Birthday

The dragon was looking forward to his birthday. He would be a thousand years old. He said to himself, "When I am a thousand years old, I will buy a thousand balloons. I will blow them all up. I will dance in the air with a thousand balloons all around me."

The night before his birthday, the dragon counted his gold. "Just enough for a thousand balloons," he said to himself, and he set off happily for his midnight swim.

Alas! While he was down on the beach, a robber crept into the cave. All the gold was stolen.

The dragon came back
and cried a thousand tears.

The next morning, a boy named Richard said to his sister, Claire, "Today's the dragon's birthday."
"Everyone knows that," said Claire.

"Poor dragon.
No one is brave enough
to go up to his cave and say
happy birthday."
"Perhaps we could go," said Richard.
"It's too dangerous," said their mother.
"He might frizzle you up."

"I've got an idea," said Claire. "We'll dress up like a dragon."

"With the dragon mask and the old red and green curtains!" said Richard. "We'll get Henry and Hannah from next door, and Billy from down the road. Then we'll go up the hill and wish the dragon a very happy birthday."

"We'll be quite safe," said Claire. "A dragon wouldn't frizzle another friendly dragon."

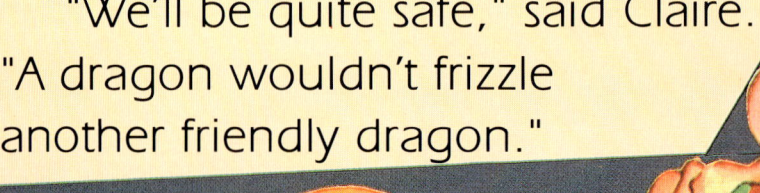

"I'll bake him a cake,"
said their mother. "A thousand-year-old
dragon deserves a treat."

Late that morning, the robber was coming down the road with the jar of stolen gold. At the same time, Richard and Claire, Henry and Hannah, and Billy were going up the road wearing their dragon costume. They looked very dragonish, except for their feet, which were in shoes and socks.

Around the corner they went. There, suddenly, they bumped into the robber. "It's a dragon!" screamed the robber in a guilty voice. "Help! Help! All is discovered! The dragons are after me!"

He was too terrified to notice the pairs of shoes. He dropped the jar of stolen gold and ran away as fast as he could.

"What was that?" said Richard, who was halfway down the dragon. "I thought I heard someone shouting."

Billy, who was wearing the mask, said, "I don't know. The mask slipped down. I couldn't see." He put the mask on straight. "Gold!" he cried. "There's a jar of gold spilled on the road!"

Hannah came out from the tail of the dragon. "It **is** gold," she said. "We've got a cake for the dragon. Now we can buy a present, too!"

"What shall we get him?" said Claire.

Henry looked out from under a curtain. "Let's visit the balloon shop. Maybe we'll get some good ideas in there."

That afternoon, the dragon sat outside his cave weeping another thousand tears. "I am a thousand years old today," he sobbed, "and all my gold is stolen. No gold. No balloons. I will have to save for another thousand years. What a long time to wait for birthday balloons!"

"Happy birthday!" called a voice. Coming up the path was a very funny dragon. It was wearing shoes and socks. It bounced and floated on the path – and no wonder! It had a thousand balloons tied to its tail.

The dragon gasped. He saw red balloons, blue balloons, green balloons and gold balloons, yellow-as-sunshine balloons, orange-as-sunset balloons, long balloons, strong balloons, curly balloons, twirly balloons.

He could not believe his dragonish eyes.

"Someone has remembered my birthday!" he cried. "Oh happy hour! Oh happy balloons! Oh happy, happy birthday!"

When Richard and Claire got home their mother said, "Did the dragon enjoy his cake?"

"He loved it," said Claire.

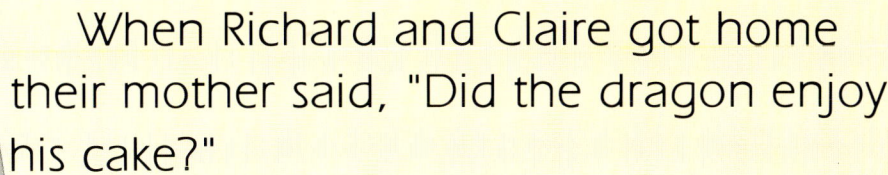

"He ate it in one mouthful, candles and all."

"Look!" Richard pointed up into the sky.

There, far up in the blue air, the dragon flew, dancing and spinning on shining wings. Around him, dancing and spinning, flew a thousand balloons, all the colors of the world.